Col. Nimrod (Mac) McNair

LEADER ☆

SHIP

☆ ☆ ☆

15 SECRETS REVEALED

Second Edition

Executive Leadership Foundation, Inc
Stone Mountain, GA

Executive Leadership Foundation Press
A division of Executive Leadership Foundation
9245 Creekside Trail
Stone Mountain, Georgia 30087-6775

Executive Leadership Foundation Press is a wholly owned division of Executive Leadership Foundation, Inc.

First Edition – Copyright 2008
Second Edition – Copyright 2011

Printed in the United States of America

Acknowledgements

The birthing of a book is a team effort. While I had the leadership experiences and put them on paper, many friends encouraged me. My wife Delysia led that team. So my personal thanks to all of you.

Endorsements

"As you know, there are certain values that we can hold true and good, and those values compel us to maintain high standards of conduct in our personal, corporate and civil life. I commend you for your commitment to excellence. It is a fine example." **George H. W. Bush**, former President of the United States.

"It is such a pleasure to see another native of our beloved Southland who also has grown up retaining and indeed revering those values which we were taught when we were boys." **Alex Haley,** the author of "Roots."

"It has been a real privilege for our city to host the first Ethics seminar which took place in Romania. We thank you and your organization for the efforts you have made in order to organize the seminar to offer the Romanian business people a real guide in business. The city hall of Ploiesti is waiting for your second seminar." **Victor Savulescu,** the Mayor of Ploiesti City, Romania.

"I have a deep concern with the lack of impact in our daily lives of the deep roots the U.S. has inherited from its Judeo-Christian beginning. I strongly endorse the work of Executive Leadership Foundation." **William S. Kanaga,** Former Chairman, U.S. Chamber of Commerce and Former Chairman, Arthur Young.

"I believe our leadership must produce standards which are articulated in written code, credos, and codes of conduct. I think it produces an environment of culture. On one hand it wants to do things right and on the other hand wants to do right things." **Donald V. Seibert**, Former Chairman of J.C. Penney Company.

"We developed a code of ethics about two years ago using materials from your organization and have found the long-term impact to be very positive. We are at an all-time high in employee morale and service. I believe that if the culture of values in an organization is right, the financial rewards will follow." **David Seim**, President and CEO, Lubbock National Bank, Lubbock, Texas.

"Some of our senior managers questioned why we were developing a code of ethics, based on your principles. They said we already do 60 – 75% of these things. But, there is something about putting it down in black and white and saying, 'This is what we believe. This is what we are committed to.' We know we can't accomplish it all the time. We are not perfect. But, unless we put a code together and say, 'This is the goal. Hold us accountable.' then we will not continue to move in that direction." **Jerry Lundquist**, Former President, Homes and Land Publishing Company, Inc.

"I have used your materials for over eight years and have found them to be an excellent tool for daily decision-making in my business and personal life. The materials are based on time-tested and proven foundational principles, and are presented in such a way that I can immediately apply them to any situation or decision that I face in daily life. They are an invaluable resource!" **Kay E. Newman**, Director of Communications, The Progress Group.

"We have a statement of values that we feel must start at the top and be deeply ingrained into the entire organization.

We have made personnel decisions based on that statement. Everyone knows we really believe in it; it isn't just a plaque on the wall. The financial situation of our company has never been better. We are substantially over-budget, debt-free and providing a better and more consistent service." **David Miller**, President and CEO, Medical Equipment Distributors, Inc.

"When I had an employee who was consistently late and absent, I used your principles as a basis for talking with him. We discussed values like individual accountability and responsibility. As a result, the employee's perspective changed, and he saw the need to fulfill his commitment to his job. His work habits have improved and he has become more productive." **Greg Rouse**, Operations Manager, Environment Control, Inc.

"I want to give Colonel McNair a word of encouragement. A lot of times you go in to speak to a group and you leave and say, 'Does this make a difference? Is it worthwhile to give my life for this?' I want to tell you that, yes, it has made a difference. The principles you present are what our Founding Fathers used to establish our country, and if a person follows them, they will be truly profitable." **Kent Humphreys**, President JACKS Service Company, Oklahoma City, Oklahoma.

Leadership
15 Secrets Revealed

Contents

Preface
Introduction

Ideas go booming through the world louder than cannons.
Thoughts are mightier than armies.
Principles have achieved more victories than horsemen or chariots.

W.M. Paxton

PREFACE

It has turned out better than I could have ever imagined.

I was born in Alabama, with crossed eyes and soon-to-be-discovered speech impediment. My parents were strong in their faith and raised five children with a very clear perspective of right and wrong. Wrong was quickly corrected with either my father's shaving strap or my mother's switch. My parents were not harsh - they loved us - but they were determined that we would be instilled with the <u>McNair standard</u>: "McNairs don't do that!"

My father was a railroad man, but he lost his job during the Great Depression, so he supported his family by farming. We learned to pull together as a family, work hard, and stay focused on sound priorities. There was no room for costly mistakes back then.

Early on, following Lindbergh's flight across the Atlantic, I knew I wanted to fly airplanes. After high school, World War II came along and I followed my childhood dream by joining the Army Air Corps.

The Army Air Corps sent me to Europe to fly P-51 Mustang fighters. I was shot down twice and survived four airplanes crashes. We flew missions over Europe escorting bombers, engaging in air-to-air combat, and strafing enemy targets. Along the way, I was awarded the Air Force Distinguished Flying Cross and other decorations. At one time, I had two hundred men reporting to me. My father and teachers had begun teaching me the principles of leadership, but I still had a long way to go. My old Master Sergeant became another teacher who had the remarkable ability to get

Col. McNair with P-51 Mustang in 1944

others to accomplish necessary objectives. Leadership was a function of his character, not his personality. I have always remembered that principle.

After the war, I finished my Bachelor of Science degree at the University of Alabama, my Master of Science degree at the Air Force Institute of Technology, and graduated from the Air Force School of Management. I studied contemporary religion for three years at the Virginia Theological Seminary and became a professor of Air Science at North Carolina State University. I served in the Korean and Vietnamese Wars flying over 100 recon missions and flew B-47 bombers with nuclear payloads along the coast of Russia during the Cold War. I was the Director of Aerospace Programs in the Pentagon, an Air Force Advisor to NASA, and a candidate for Governor in the state of Georgia.

I am currently the President of the McNair Group, a

business-consulting firm, and Chairman as well as the Founder of the Executive Leadership Foundation, a non-profit organization that promotes ethics in business and society based on Judeo-Christian values. I am a Certified Management Consultant and am listed in the "Dictionary of International Biographies" and "Who's Who in America." My speaking audience includes countless Governors' and Mayors' prayer breakfasts, business meetings and seminars in over 75 countries on the subjects of management and leadership. I have written five books: *Absolute Ethics*, *Leadership, Mega Values, Ten Principles for Marriage,* and *Leadership: A Study of Time-Proven Principles.* In my last leadership position, I had the responsibility for 2,000 people plus a $2 billion budget.

Enough about me. Let's talk about how you can improve your leadership skills by using the 15 Secrets.

SECRETS

A secret is something not known or seen or not meant to be known or seen by others. Many keys to leadership have been a secret for far too long. This book is about decoding leadership secrets for everyone.

Some secrets are protected for decades or even centuries. I played a role in a few of America's best-kept secrets. In order to provide leadership instruction, I will now for the first time reveal details of a national Top Secret on the next few pages! In a later chapter I will disclose another mostly declassified, though still almost unknown, USA Top Secret. Rev your engines. Wheels up. We are going for a high-speed, high-altitude leadership tour like no other. Enjoy the ride!

National Top Secret Story #1

The original Star Wars Defense.

During the Cold War, after the Sputnik satellite was launched in 1957, it became clear that the USSR might be able to rain down nuclear destruction on the United States. I was a flight test pilot, had a Masters in Aerospace Engineering and had the qualifications to be an astronaut. I was not selected for no other reason than they had more people than they needed and so I was given a job as a technical advisor to NASA, but the primary role that I had was clandestine missions. One was called "Program 437" which was to come up with a defense system to shoot down the Soviet satellite, Sputnik, when it was first put up. I formed a team with members of Douglas aircraft, resulting in the 10th Aerospace Defense Squadron. Our project was top secret. This required me to perform as though I was not even in the Air Force. We developed a system that we placed on Johnston Island located six to seven hundred miles south of Hawaii. We put a nuclear missile on a Thor missile. About every ninety minutes, Sputnik circled the earth and passed over Johnston Island at a low altitude. If

 we had found it necessary, we could have shot it down. Our missile became operational as a weapons system as a result of that. The 10th Aerospace Squadron was formed within the Air Defense Command and the Air Defense Command became the Aerospace Defense Command.

The program was completely unknown to the US public until the fall of 1964, when during an election campaign President Lyndon Johnson disclosed the existence of the anti-satellite system. Personally, I considered this to be a poor example of leadership because it exposed our defense ability to our potential enemies. The Tenth Aerospace Defense Squadron, or "Program 437", was terminated in 1973.

During "Program 437," I lived in California and I would fly to Hawaii, and then down to Johnston Island. No one knew where I was. My wife wasn't sure whether I was still in the Air Force or not. But once that program became operational and since I was a systems planner for the program, I received a commendation from the Secretary of the Air Force. It was a memorandum in which I was complimented by Secretary Eugene Zuckert, who was a very interesting personality - I admired him greatly. Of course people didn't know why I got it because they didn't know what I was doing!

Sometimes you do things without any compensation because of the nature of what you're doing, or sometimes you get delayed compensation for it. In this particular case, I received a memorandum from the Secretary of the Air Force, and everyone was wondering, "Why did McNair get that? What did he do?"

DEPARTMENT OF THE AIR FORCE
WASHINGTON

OFFICE OF THE SECRETARY
February 17, 1964

MEMORANDUM FOR THE CHIEF OF STAFF

It was a pleasure to receive the attached memorandum from Dr. Charles M. Herzfeld, Deputy Director of the Advanced Research Projects Agency, complimenting Major Nimrod McNair of SSD for his contribution in the development of a detailed study of the technical potential for developing a non-nuclear kill anti-satellite weapon system.

Please convey my compliments to Major McNair for the recognition he has gained for himself and the Air Force.

Eugene M. Zuckert

Attachment

cc: Vice Chief of Staff

Leadership Secret 1

LEADERSHIP IS FOR EVERYONE

People think at the top there isn't much room.

They tend to think of it as an Everest.

My message is that there is tons

of room at the top.

Margaret Thatcher

W ithout leadership there can be no success in life. Who then should lead?" Everyone! Children lead everyday—at home with siblings, on the playground, on sports teams and in school plays. Parents lead children from infancy through early adulthood. People in virtually every honorable profession can and do lead— sometimes more effectively than their bosses—as we will learn, position does not make a leader.

The only difference from one accomplished leader to another should be scale. Some will lead a few people, some dozens and others hundreds or thousands. The parent who properly supplies timeless leadership principles to parenting is no less a leader than the CEO of a major company or even President of a nation. Only the number of followers is different.

Leadership—15 Secrets Revealed defines complete leadership so you will know how to identify the complete leaders and become one yourself. If you are already a complete leader, you may still discover truth and insights to help you further improve your skills and life. The world's best athletes and performers routinely return to fundamentals. This book is full of leadership fundamentals that work for leaders on every level.

Regardless of race, color, creed or ethnic background, leaders are all subject to fundamental laws and some moral compass to live by. History says that the Decalogue that Moses brought down off the mountain top is mankind's best moral compass. The application of these principles in the business world is more profitable, in government more effective, and in education the very foundation for all disciplines. There are absolute principles that are still mankind's best moral compass. God gave us these principles to live and lead a more effective life regardless of the institution that we are a part of.

Carefully chosen quotes have been placed through this leadership manual to inspire you in your quest for leadership greatness. Please take time to absorb the wisdom from these leaders, thinkers and authors. If just one quote spurs you to action, your leadership IQ and life will be enriched.

Remember: leadership is for everyone and is taught by our mentors. Here are four of my mentors:

Lead, follow, or get the hell out of the way!

General George S. Patton,
Third Army, WWII

Captain (McNair), you're the aircraft commander. The decision is yours to make.

General Curtis LeMay,
Commander, Strategic Air Command

When you have looked thoroughly into a problem and come to certain conclusions, you must have the courage to stand up and fight for them. You should not be influenced by whether your point of view is popular or not.

Dr. Frederik Philips,
CEO, Philips Corporation

Some of the best business and nonprofit CEOs I've worked with over a sixty-five year consulting career were not stereotypical leaders. They were all over the map in terms of their personalities, attitudes, values, strengths, and weaknesses.

Peter Drucker
International author and consultant on
Business Management Theory and Practice

Leadership Secret 2

LEAD PEOPLE, MANAGE THINGS

Love people. Use things.

Original Author Unknown

*Popularized by Arthur S. DeMoss
Chairman and Founder of
National Liberty Corporation*

People should be led, not managed! That's right. Many tasks and jobs do require supervision and everyone—including major CEOs and sports superstars—require coaching. Yet people are often over-supervised and over-managed. Have you ever heard of a child, company or project being "over-led?" People intuitively hunger for more leadership, not more management. We are made to be led and to lead others.

What then should be managed? Time, plans, budgets and all types of things. Lead people. Manage things. It works. Try it!

Definition of Leadership

Leadership is getting something accomplished through others. Leadership is the process of inspiring one or more individuals to strive for and reach a specific goal or objective.

A leader is someone who knows where he is going and has someone following him. Some leaders know where they are going but no one is following them—other leaders have followers but they do not know where they are going.

A leader is not a sideline observer, but a mover and a shaker. The familiar phrase, "Follow me!" pretty well expresses the behavior of an effective leader. A leader is someone who does not have to use extrinsic motivation (leader implies, "do it or else") but develops an intrinsic motivation (follower thinks, "I want to follow you").

A good leader does not draw attention to himself. *Chinese Leader Lao-Tz* said, "A leader is best when people barely know that he exists." A good leader who talks little—when his work is

done and aim fulfilled—will motivate followers to say, "We did this ourselves."

Some people confuse the direction of leadership—they think it is always from the top down. Effective leadership is three dimensional: up, down and collateral.

Up—You may be the CEO, but you will have to answer to a Board of Directors. The Board answers to the company's shareholders.

Down—This is the commonly recognized scenario where you have a group of people that report to you.

Collateral—You are the leader of your group, but you have to work with the leaders of other groups in the organization. To be an effective leader, you must recognize different relationships and treat each one with the appropriate respect and work toward the common goal.

The Different roles of Leaders & Managers

Unfortunately, our educational system develops managers but not necessarily leaders. There is a big difference between managers and leaders.

Managers are concerned about the efficiency of the effort while leaders are concerned about the effectiveness of the effort. For example, in a military situation the commander will be concerned more about winning the battle, the manager will be worried more about what supplies and manpower it will take to win the battle.

A leader will get to the top of the mountain with resources depleted. A manager will get just half way up the mountain with resources still intact.

Leadership & Management Relationship

Success comes when both effective management and dynamic leadership exist within the organization. Keep in mind: all of the principles in this book apply to individuals and families as well as every form of group or organization.

Decision-making, problem-analysis, planning and organizing are managerial skills. These skills are highly necessary, even though they are not always leadership skills. Leaders must have all these skills, but they are not the most important undertaking that leaders do. Leaders *must* think, have a vision, set the course and standards and inspire others to join the leader's cause, therefore accomplishing specific goals. Leaders must lead!

A good manager makes decisions daily and must not be lacking in this skill, or the whole process, whether manufacturing, sales or service, will bog down. Often managers get "analysis paralysis" or have other challenges that stall progress; it is then the leader's role to have a bias for action to make sure things get done.

Problem analysis involves a clear assessment of all the potential pitfalls and how they can be avoided through careful planning and meticulous monitoring of resources, business activities, the competition and other factors. Problem analysis must be ongoing to divert organizational setbacks.

Planning is determining how the goals and objectives can be accomplished in a given time period. Once you have the plan, you organize. Organizing requires unity of command. Unity of command means one boss. You cannot serve two masters.

I was fortunate to have been trained in both leadership skills as well as management skills. I had the opportunity to practice them by leading men over the target in wartime, managing aerospace programs in the Air Force, advising NASA and advising clients as an international management consultant.

After my tour in Vietnam, I went into the business world. I was somewhat surprised by the lack of emphasis on leadership skills. Managerial skills were and remain center stage at business schools, in corporations and government.

Harvard University initiated the MBA program in 1921. Since that time, emphasis has been on management at the expense of leadership. I have observed MBAs coming in at the middle of the organizational structure and wanting to go up. Leaders start at the bottom and go up.

Management by objectives was a fad in the 1980s. Management by purpose is what works. Management by objectives is from the top down. Leadership by purpose is from the bottom up. While leaders establish vision and purpose, everyone shares in that purposeful vision.

Leaders and managers complement each other and their functions are both necessary for the success of an organization. Character and a strong moral compass are necessary in both positions. In some smaller companies, both the role of leader and manager are by necessity exercised by the same person. In all instances, we must manage ourselves and allow others to spread their wings and lead.

Leadership is the lifting of a man's vision to higher sights, the raising of a man's performance to a higher standard, the building of a man's personality beyond its normal limitations.

Peter Drucker
The Practice of Management, 1955

Don't tell people how to do things, tell them what to do and let them surprise you with the results.

General George S. Patton

Leadership Secret 3

LEADERS ARE MADE, NOT BORN

It is the height of absurdity
to sow little but weeds
in the first half of one's lifetime
and expect to harvest a valuable crop
in the second half.

Percy H. Johnson
President of Chemical Bank

Make no mistake about it: leadership is learned—a person is not born with it. You can improve your leadership skills dramatically and successfully through study, application and mentoring—all will be covered in the chapters to follow.

A leader has four tools:
1. **Position.**   This is by assignment.
2. **Competence.** Acquired through learning and training.
3. **Personality.** What people think we are.
4. **Character.**   Who we really are—our pattern of behavior.

Character is by far the most important and effective tool of all. We teach in military leadership courses: "The most important attributes of a military leader in a democratic society are character, honesty and integrity." But character is something that requires some value source or standard. Consequently, each of us has used some source: our parents, teachers, employers, our morals and faith.

Historically, leaders of character, creativity, motivation, and conviction have been nurtured by values and standards modeled in the home. These individuals pioneered change and reached levels of achievement that have benefited mankind in virtually every discipline.

Personalities with values that can specifically be traced to their home education include: Presidents George Washington and Abraham Lincoln, inventors Thomas Edison and the Wright Brothers, and figures from history such as Winston Churchill, Patrick Henry, Sandra Day O'Connor, Pearl Buck, C.S. Lewis, George Washington Carver, Albert Schweitzer, Andrew Carnegie, Claude Monet, General Douglas MacArthur, General George

Patton, Moses, John Wesley and Jesus of Nazareth. There are countless others. You would be wise to read the biographies of these leaders.

Character is developed over a lifetime and it is never too late to improve our character. The stronger our character, the better we are prepared for all of life's leadership challenges.

Leaders are made, they are not born. Leaders are made when parents teach their children and their children's children. Those principles of leadership and character have been in existence from the beginning of mankind, and they are just as true and reliable today.

To bring oneself to a frame of mind and to the proper energy to accomplish things that require plain hard work continuously is the one big  **battle that everyone has. When this battle is won for all time, then everything is easy.**

Thomas A. Buckner

All great changes in America begin at the dinner table.

Ronald Reagan

The average, normal man who is fitted into the uniform of an American ground soldier is what his home, his religion, his schooling, and the moral code and ideals of his society have made him, The Army cannot unmake him.

General George C. Marshal

The success of the commander does not arise from following rules or models. It consists of an absolute new comprehension of the dominant facts of the situation at the time and all the forces at work.

Winston Churchill

Winston Churchill – July 1944
Taken by Mac McNair in Cherbourg, France

Never, never, never quit.

Winston Churchill

It is not enough that we do our best; sometimes we have to do what's required.

Winston Churchill

Leadership Secret 4

THE POWER OF INDIVIDUALS

Two roads diverged in a wood,

and I—I took the one less traveled by,

and that has made all the difference.

Robert Frost

Institutions do not change the world. Individuals do. There are few statutes erected to institutions or companies and there is not one statute honoring a committee.

Leadership is the life-blood in all of our institutions: business, nonprofit, government, education and faith. Without leaders, the future of our institutions is in peril. So, we call for leadership, not to the society of institutions, but to individuals who are willing to pay the price to lead.

Promoting the power of the individual does not mean neglecting teamwork! The theme and principle serves to remind us that teams are collections of individuals. Communism was, and remains in some places, an attempt to strip individuals of their uniqueness and their rights— citizens become mere servants to the almighty state and taskmaster. Organizations must always understand that the specialness and power over every person is the core of teamwork and group success. It is the leader's challenge to empower individuals and motivate them to work together.

There is no institution that demands more of its leaders than the military, because freedom is not free. In the founding of this country, of the fifty-six men who signed  the Declaration of Independence in which they committed themselves, their lives and their duties—most of them gave their lives. Individuals, not institutions, make the ultimate sacrifice.

Are you as a leader allowing those around you to shine as individuals? Are you encouraging others in your family, group or organization to be leaders?

A modern leader I met is Jesse Ventura, the 38th Governor of Minnesota.

I was speaking at a prayer breakfast in a little town just north of Minnesota, and I said, "Will the mayor be here?" A man said, "Yes, there he is now. He's coming in the door." I was sitting at the head table at the time and as I looked at the door, he was wearing a bandanna and had a t-shirt on. He was a big, burly individual and I said, "Is that the mayor?" They said, "Yeah, that's the mayor."

He came up, greeted me, and then sat down at the table. When he got up to speak to the people, he talked just like he looked in that old bandana and t-shirt. He was a former wrestler and had been at the gym. He gazed out at the crowd in the room and said, "I know you guys elected me as the mayor of this town. Now you want me to do this and you want me to do that and you want this and that. Well, I've got news for you. The mayor and the staff can't do all that." He took his big finger and said, "You and you and you are the ones that have to do it."

Institutions don't change society, individuals do.

Remember always that you not only have the right to be an individual, you have an obligation to be one.

Eleanor Roosevelt

35

You miss 100 percent of the shots you never take.

Wayne Gretzky

If you think you can or think you can't, you're probably right.

Mark Twain

Do not wait for leaders; do it alone, person to person.

Mother Teresa

Some men see things as they are and say "Why?'
I dream things that never were and say 'Why not?'

George Bernard Shaw

Leadership Secret 5

UNITY OF PURPOSE

A man without a purpose

is like a ship without a rudder.

Thomas Carlyle

O n May 25, 1961, President John F. Kennedy boldly challenged America to set sail on what he later called, "the most hazardous and greatest *adventure on which man has ever embarked."*

"I believe that this nation should commit itself to achieving the goal, before this decade is out, of landing a man on the moon and returning him safely to the Earth."

JFK told America the importance in UNITY OF PURPOSE. "But in a very real sense, it will not be one man going to the moon—if we make this judgment affirmatively, it will be an entire nation. For all of us must work to put him there."

I had the honor of being part of the Apollo Space program. It was a great experience and most enjoyable and educational to work for leaders like Dr. Edward Teller.

On July 24, the Pacific Ocean welcomed a terrific splash from the command capsule, heralding the safe return of three new heroes for a world that would be forever changed. Mission accomplished!

The basic principle that produces productivity and harmony is the unity of purpose principle. This occurs when people work together with a common purpose and common goals. Unity of purpose is always based on a specific value system or norm. When the value system is not followed, the process is disrupted and problems arise.

Diversity of purpose is the root of disaster. One cause of trouble: we have deviated from being a law-based society whose success is dependent on the rationale of personal responsibility and accountability.

Having different opinions by team members is healthy, normal and desirable because it adds to the possibility of finding the correct direction. The leader must go through a decision making process that will determine the best alternative. It's like buying a house. You list the objectives that you want to accomplish: schools, churches, business and then you look at the various alternatives available. You evaluate them against the criteria you have established and one of those alternatives will best satisfy the criteria. When you do the risk analysis, you ask yourself, "What could go wrong? What is the probability it could go wrong, and how serious will it be?" The probability of going wrong can be 90% or it could be 10% and you have to make a decision on the basis of whether you want to take the risk or not.

However, in the end, unity of purpose wins the day every day. Is everyone on your team unified with a single purpose? If not, why not? Are you the one to boldly and clearly cast the vision and purpose as JFK did? Maybe your team or organization has been derailed; are you the leader to get your train back on track? Go ahead, you can do it!

Impress upon the mind of every man from the highest to the lowest the importance of the cause they are contending for.

General George Washington

The time is always right to do what is right.

Dr. Martin Luther King, Jr.

Leadership Secret 6

HISTORY IS PROFITABLE

Today a reader,

tomorrow a leader.

W. Fusselman

T o become a good leader, you must become a student of history and the key players that shaped nations and cultures. When you allocate time to read about individuals who have changed the world, you will be rewarded.

This book is not designed to exclude anyone as a leader. The principles herein are for everyone. In history, because of societal structures, men were almost always the recognized leaders of those times and therefore the historical leaders we know the most about.

I believe when we went West in a covered wagon and women pulled out a rifle and fought the redskins just like the men did and worked hard on the ranches and homesteads, that things began to change. In World War II, women took on the traditional working roles of men in our manufacturing plants because our men were away at war. They did a great job and have never left. You cannot put a gender adjective in front of the noun leadership. When you do, you have told a lie. Leadership is leadership is leadership, regardless of race, color, creed or gender.

I admire Margaret Thatcher very much. She served with distinction as the first woman Prime Minister of England for eleven years, the third longest term of any Prime Minister. She was known for her character and conviction by  revitalizing Britain's economy, impacting the trade unions, and re-establishing the nation as a world power. While she had many critics and her position was not easy, she stayed the course. Upon her eventual death, she is to be honored with a state funeral at St Paul's Cathedral, the first prime minister to be so honored since Sir Winston Churchill in 1965.

Down through history and throughout the world, women have had positions of leadership and have accomplished exceptional goals for their people. Records show as early as 2,500 BC there was an Egyptian queen who was in power. In our own country, women are currently serving with distinction as heads of businesses, mayors, governors and members of Congress.

World-changing Leadership

History demonstrates that individual characters that are committed to absolute values, can have an indelible influence on the course of events. William Wilberforce was one such individual. A member of the English Parliament in the early 1800's and  noted for his vigorous leadership, he spearheaded the passage of the historic bill outlawing slavery in the British Empire. In 1807, Wilberforce and a coalition of friends skilled in national and international politics, business and law, began working to legally abolish slavery. For over twenty years, they continued their diligent work of writing, speaking and gathering public support against slavery. The law was finally passed in 1833. They not only changed the law but also the practice of slavery in the mind-set of the people, which contradicted the interest of big business. Such leadership of character was missing in the country's very foundation. One man changed the positive course of history.

Leadership in Crisis

In 1982 seven people died after taking cyanide-laced Tylenol. To prevail in the crisis, Johnson and Johnson relied on its standards (instituted in 1947 and revised in 1979). **"Our credo challenges us to put the needs and well-being of the people we serve, first."** The credo played the single most important role in the decision-

making process according to their Chairman James Burk. Their standard of ethics was the unifying force with many executives making critical decisions, independent of any written emergency procedures. Had *J & J* not responded to its credo, the entire company would have run headlong into financial disaster.

Leadership Conviction & Courage

Another example of dedicated leadership: When confronted by the Japanese in World War II to take down

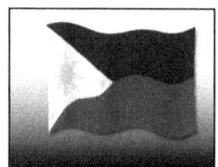

the American Flag and the Filipino Flag, the Filipino college president refused to do it. They shot and wounded him. As he lay there, his secretary came running to him asking, "Why, why did you refuse to do so?" He made one of the most powerful statements of personal integrity and leadership I have ever heard:

> *"There comes a time in every person's life when they must both certify and seal by their behavior that which they say they believe."*

Did you get that? *"We* must both certify and seal by *our* behavior that which *we* say *we* believe." Since the beginning of mankind, we have seen those times come in our lives. How we respond determines leadership.

Leadership based on moral character, has been closely associated with captains of industry throughout history. J.C. Penney personally built his business on the golden rule of treating employees and customers, as he would want to be treated. The J.C. Penney stores were often referred to as the "Golden Rule stores."

Not unlike Penney, Milton S. Hershey built the Hershey Corporation in 1903 on the values synonymous with his own lifestyle of integrity, industry, benefits to others, family and community. These values drove the company and still identify and invisibly have given the company staying power after 110 years.

In the business world, James Cash Penney, James Dole of Dole Pineapple, and C.E. Woolman, the founder of Delta Airlines, are examples of leaders who  consistently demonstrated strong, uncompromising moral character. Quick: when you think of "golden rule leaders" today, who comes to mind? Could there be a shortage? Maybe you are such a leader and if so, congratulations.

The best thing you can do is pass your complete leadership on to those around you and to your family.

While we can all learn from great, complete leaders in history, leaders from the past cannot lead today and tomorrow. That is up to us.

Moral cowardice that keeps us from speaking our minds is as dangerous to this country as irresponsible talk. The right way is not always the popular and easy way.

Standing for right when it is unpopular is a true test of moral character.

Margaret Chase Smith
First woman to be elected
to both houses of Congress.

Character is higher than intellect.

Ralph Waldo Emerson

Be always sure you're right, then go ahead.

Davy Crockett

Leadership Secret 7

THE MORAL COMPASS

The supreme quality for a leader
is unquestionable integrity.
Without it, no real success is possible,
no matter whether it is on a section gang,
a football field,
in an army or in an office.

Dwight D. Eisenhower

O ne of the biggest leadership lies many have come to accept: the personal values of an individual have little bearing on his public performance or credibility as a leader. In fact, the opposite is true. Dwight Eisenhower had it right: "Development of one's character is the single most important ingredient for a successful leader."

The Moral Compass Develops at Home

The ultimate key to leadership is the moral compass that is taught to the child or person as they go through the cycle of life. This teaching needs to begin in the home. We all know the foundational education principle: "Parents, teach your children and your children's children." Someone has to teach character.

In every nation on earth, the fundamental unit of society is a man, woman and child. In this family unit, the responsibility for teaching character rests with the parents. The child's character will be no better than the character of the parents (after years of heartache and trials, the child can develop character traits his parents lacked). That's why legacy and heritage are so important.

Home is the place where you teach your youngster everything, from the law of gravity to their spoken language. Most important, home is the place to teach your child a character standard that will produce a leader. Then the child will lead based on character and not personality.

Four Value Systems—Choose Carefully

Character is a function of the value system an individual is taught. There are four types of value systems:

1. **Traditional values system:**
   My parents did it that way, my grandparents did it that way, so it has to be right.
2. **Situational ethics values system:**
   If it feels good, do it.
3. **Rambo values system:**
   It's going to be done my way.
4. **Synthesizing values system:**
   Develop character relative to some standard that has proven to be effective down through the ages.
   This is the system that works best.

If the best character is one that is synthesized, then how do you find the basis for the synthesis? For more than three thousand years, we have found a moral compass that history proves is mankind's moral compass. We find evidence of this moral compass in every culture on planet earth. How does a young child anywhere in the world know he is lying or stealing? Most call this CONSCIENCE.

Why does man not use that moral compass if it produces the character necessary for building leadership? The answer is very simple: inherent within mankind, regardless of his culture, his birth, or family background, is an element that has to be dealt with to effectively use the moral compass. That element is the fundamental flaw in mankind: it is called pride. It is a characteristic that most effective leaders struggle with. Their ability to overcome that negative element is a key to leadership. Some people refer to it as "servanthood leadership:" willingness to serve others rather than to be served. Others refer to it as "a cause-oriented character."

I think it is a function of the principles of the universe. For example: the law of gravity. Regardless of race, color, creed, ethnic background, etc., if you jump off a fifty-story building, you are going to hit the ground. A former student  of mine was a program manager on the F-22 airplane built by Lockheed. I said to him, "I know 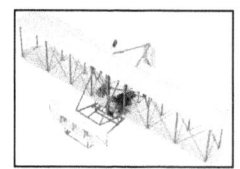 you won't be using the Wright Brothers' principles of flight to build this airplane." He said, "Of course we will or we will crash off the end of the runway!"

Leadership principles have been established for as long as the law of gravity. Those character-building principles must be taught and must start at the top. The leader must have principles in his own life before he can expect others to follow. We had a saying in the Air Force about a fighter pilot who had a wingman: "If you can't trust your wingman with your wife, you better not trust him with your life." You need a moral compass to fly by.

Will we make mistakes as a leader? Of course we will. That's why we cannot delegate the principles of leadership. Character is the most important principle. I think the military made a mistake when they made the Chaplain responsible for character-building. It should be the responsibility of the Commander. The business world made a mistake when it passed the ethics responsibility off to Human Resources.

Former Chairman of the U.S. Chamber of Commerce, Bill Kanaga, said, "It is an inviolable truth that ethics must start at the top."

Tom Hamilton, former Attorney General of California said, "If the moral compass isn't at the top, then the arch has no keystone."

Unfortunately, many of our institutions become utter disasters and are unable to fulfill their responsibility because they do not have a leader who is the moral compass. Both the leader and the manager must have a moral compass.

Difference between Legal and Right

One of leadership's grandest failures is thinking, "If something is legal it must be okay." Many people and companies do things that are completely legal, yet completely wrong and unethical. Being legal is not the same as being right! Of course we must all obey the laws of the land, but that is not enough. We must also always behave with high ethical and moral standards. Scores of companies have allowed lawyers to essentially have final say on all controversial or uncertain corporate actions— they report back to management, "It is legal, so go ahead and do it if you want to". Once again, it is the leader's job to set and enforce the standard of values, character and behavior.

Behave Right, Make More Money!

There is evidence that those who behave ethically and morally towards their various constituencies are those that make the most money. The Ethics Resource Center in Washington, D.C. (www.ethics.org) has found companies with a written commitment to social responsibility financially outperform companies without such a code or a standard over an extended period of time.

The best leaders are made, not born, and they are built as they study, understand and recognize the principles of the universe. Most importantly, we must not lose sight of the moral compass we all have within us—the inner sense of right and wrong that helps us build strong character, essential for all of life's leadership challenges.

A reputation for a thousand years may depend upon the conduct of a single moment.

Ernest Bramah

Whenever you are to do a thing, though it can never be known but to yourself, ask how you would act were all the world looking at you and act accordingly.

Thomas Jefferson

Let us raise a standard to which the wise and honest may repair. The rest is in the hands of God.

George Washington

The image of George Washington kneeling in prayer at Valley Forge says something about the method of all leadership—humble, modest service.

George Sweeting

Character is what you are in the dark.

Dwight L. Moody

The higher type of man clings to virtue; the lower type of man clings to material comfort. The

higher type of man cherishes justice; the lower type of man cherishes the hope of favors received.

Confucius, Chinese philosopher

All that is required for evil to triumph is for good men to do nothing.

Sir Edmond Burke

When there is moral rot within a nation, its government topples easily, but with honest sensible leaders, there is stability.

Proverbs 11:14

When a country is rebellious, it has many rulers, but a man of understanding and knowledge maintains order.

Proverbs 28:2

Leadership Secret 8

LEADERS ARE WINNERS ... AND KNOW HOW TO LOSE

I am not concerned that you have fallen;
I am concerned that you arise.

Abraham Lincoln

Personally, I have lost many times, but leaders always "fly over the target" even if they get shot down. Some decisions do not always end with the success you had hoped, but you make your best judgment and see it through.

During the Battle of the Bulge in WWII, I was asked to fly out President Roosevelt's son's airplane. Elliot

Roosevelt ran out of fuel in his P-38 Lockheed Lightning and landed it near Luxemburg City on a par 5 golf course, which fortunately was straight and did not have a dogleg. We were asked to send our crews there to look after the airplane until the engineers could come in and build a temporary runway or dismantle the airplane and take it out. It was about that time that the Germans began to approach Bastogne. Everyone got very upset about what was going to happen to the crew members and the maintenance fellows. My squadron commander asked me if I could go down and see what was going on and maybe fly it out.

I got in my jeep with my driver, a young fellow from New York, an Italian kid named DeMarco. We headed south from Liege, Belgium to Luxemburg City. We went straight through Bastogne and straight through the Battle of the Bulge. We did not even know it had started, because no one else knew it either. When we arrived in Luxemburg City, it was late at night and we went into a hotel that was

operated by the army. The sergeant said, "You can have a room if you need it." And I said, "Fine, good." About that time a major walked into the hotel and said, "Hold every room in the hotel. General Patton and his staff will be here shortly." General Patton was south of there and when the Battle of the Bulge started, he took off, headed up to support the operation and had to come through Luxemburg City. When the major said hold all rooms in the hotel, I said, "I gotta have a room." The major said, "Alright, give the lieutenant a room." I was a big second lieutenant, and so I got a room. The next day, I fortunately had dinner with General Patton and his staff. They had plenty of turkeys because the turkeys had been sent to the 7th Army, who had all been captured by the Germans, so the turkeys were diverted to where we were. After that I decided I had better go and see what we could do about getting that airplane out.

Meanwhile, there was plenty of snow on the ground, about eight or twelve inches. The Battle of the Bulge was underway because when I got to where my crew people and the airplane were, you could hear the guns going off. These guys were all frightened because they were Army Air Corps and they did not know much about guns and shooting.

So I took a look, and I thought I had 800 feet where I could take the P-38 off. Meanwhile, they had stripped it of everything - the radios, you name it, anything not needed was not on the airplane. So I told them, "Lock the airplane, right here at the T, where you start your golf game and I'll push the throttles all the way forward. When the turbos cut in, I'll turn her lose. I want two of you guys to be 800 feet down on the fairway. When I get there, wave a flag and I'll know it's time to take off."

I did not have any perforated runway or anything, just snow on the fairway because the engineers were unable to do anything. As I locked the breaks and pushed the throttles all the way forward, the P-38 would slide off to one side or the other. So finally, I had them dig a hole so the wheels would go right down into the dirt. I knew I had to get the weight off the gear before I could take off because the gear would not come up if you did not get the weight off of it. So I finally got the throttles all forward, locked the breaks, the turbos cut in and I turned her loose. Boy, we took off down that fairway, but what I did not think about was the snow. The props blew the snow up in the air and I could not see those guys down on the fairway with their flags, so I had to guess where to take off. Later, they told me that I lifted off exactly on the money.

The airplane took off like a homesick angel. At about 100 feet off the ground, one engine quit on me, because the airplane had been sitting for about fifty days and the lubricants were clogged. As I flew over the German lines, they started shooting at me, so I dropped the airplane down to an even lower altitude and rolled the P-38 to try and get away from the German lines. About that time, they shot out the other engine. Fortunately, I was able to restart the first engine and put the fire out on the second, avoiding having to bail out. I rolled her around and came back over our lines and was able to fly on up to Liege, Belgium.

I thought, "Boy, I'm going to be a hero for salvaging the President's son's airplane!" But when I came into Liege to land on another short runway, I did not have any radio contact with the tower, so they signaled me with a green light to land. When I came in to land and touched down, I realized that the airplane was going off to the left. What I did not know was the Germans had shot out the landing gear lock on the left side of the airplane and of course the gear was just swinging. The guys in the mobile tower saw me coming toward them and they were jumping out and running like crazy. I was able to bounce the airplane and get the other gear up, but it went off into the ditch and unfortunately the airplane was pretty much totaled. I was OK, but I did not turn out to be a hero after all.

The Allies went on to win the Battle of the Bulge without me. Victory in Europe occurred three months later.

Leaders are winners. And they know how to lose… and lose… and lose. Consider the amazing record of Abraham Lincoln, America's 16th President.

Lost job, 1832
Defeated for legislature, 1832
Failed in business, 1833
Elected to legislature, 1834
Sweetheart (Ann Rutledge) died, 1835
Had nervous breakdown, 1836
Defeated for Speaker, 1838
Defeated for nomination for Congress, 1843
Elected to Congress, 1846
Lost re-nomination, 1848
Rejected for Land Officer, 1849
Defeated for Senate, 1854
Defeated for nomination of Vice President, 1856
Again defeated for Senate, 1858
Elected President, 1860

Lincoln went on to build a life of accomplishments out of defeats.

Winston Churchill instructed, "Even ordinary life and business involve the encountering of unknown factors and require some effort of the imagination, some stress of the soul, to overcome them."

How do you deal with "stress of the soul"? Absorb wisdom from the next few pages.

I was a candidate for Governor of Georgia at the age of 70. I lost, but I won in many ways. I became well known throughout the State for my leadership experiences and principles, especially ethics. Leaders do not quit.

The great question is not whether you have failed, but whether you are content in failure.

William Shakespeare

The credit belongs to the man who is actually in the arena, whose face is marred by dust and sweat and blood, who strives valiantly, who errs and comes short again and again, who knows the great enthusiasms, the great devotions, and spends himself in a worthy cause, who at best knows achievement and who at the worst if he fails at least fails while daring greatly so that his place shall never be with those cold and timid souls who know neither victory nor defeat.

Theodore Roosevelt

Leadership Secret 9

RELATIONSHIP HARMONY

Learning is acquired by reading books,
but the much more necessary learning,
the knowledge of the world,
is only to be acquired by reading men,
and studying all the various facets of them.

Lord Chesterfield

G etting along with others is paramount for all leaders. It is also important for *everyone* in a group of any size—from three in a family to hundreds of thousands in the world's largest organizations—to understand and benefit from the principles of relationship harmony.

What if we all actually tried to show love, kindness, justice, concern, respect, trust, fairness and generosity to all? Jesus of Nazareth offered, "Love your neighbor as yourself." Until the utopian time when everyone applies this advice, we must deal with the human condition and the extraordinary complexity of human behavior.

Early in my career I was a student at Lehigh University studying Group Dynamics. This is where I learned to understand the personalities we are born with that govern our behavioral styles.

1. **High control personality:**
   If you get three or four of these people together, you have got a fist-fight looking for a place to happen.
2. **Influence personality:**
   If you get several of these people together, you have got a party looking for a place to happen.
3. **Steady, dependable personality:**
   If you get three or four of these folks together, you have got a great team, but no leader.
4. **Compliance personality:**
   With several of these people together, you have an accounting firm.

If we function only on our high control personality, we wind up with a dictatorship. If we use only our influence personality, we wind up with a great bunch of guys, but nothing will be accomplished. If we have a leader with a steady, dependable personality, no one will know who is in charge. Finally, if we have a compliance type personality who thinks that two-plus-two equals 4.00000, we will be constantly correcting, but achieving little.

A remarkable phenomenon: you can identify the individual personality profiles of an individual while he is still in the crib. This is why it is so important that character building starts as early as possible. Consider:

1. **High control personality:**
   He is standing in his crib rattling the bars—he wants out. He wants to do what he wants to do.
2. **Influence personality:**
   She'll be talking at night while you are trying to sleep. She'll talk to her teddy bear, she'll talk to the ceiling, she'll just talk…talk…talk.
3. **Steady dependable personality:**
   He will be lying there in his crib happily smiling, even though he has not been fed and his diaper is wet.
4. **Compliance personality:**
   She wants to be fed thirty seconds before feeding time and wants her diaper changed thirty seconds before she wets it.

Around 60 A.D., Paul of Tarsus had a pretty good track record in building men. He said in a letter to Timothy, "To inspire leadership is a noble ambition." Then he gave four important characteristics of an effective leader:

1.	A man of self-discipline
2.	A good relationship with his wife
3.	A well behaved family
4.	A good reputation

Three of these four things involve relationship harmony and the first item—self-discipline—involves self-understanding. While the Apostle Paul's prescription for how to spot a leader is wise advice, there is much more to identifying leaders and people destined for success.

Peter Drucker said, "Executives make poor staffing and promotion decisions. By all accounts, their batting average is no better than .333: at most one-third of such decisions turn out right; one third are minimally effective and one-third are outright failures."

The two main reasons people leave jobs are:
1) They were not in a job well suited for them to start with, and
2) They cannot get along with one or more people.
Human judgment and conventional "testing" have failed to sufficiently solve this problem.

Why is this so important? Remember our leadership definition: "Leadership is getting something accomplished through others. Leadership is the process of inspiring one or more individuals to reach a specific goal or objective." Leadership is all about people! Communicating with people. Software has transformed almost every area of our lives and soon it will be able to greatly advance our personal relationships, work relationships, career and organizational success. However, one-on-one communication still inspires people the most.

How much attention are you paying to the importance of people and relationships? Don't ever lose sight of every leader's greatest asset: people such as our team, our mentors and coaches, our associates and of course our followers. All are real people with real heartbeats and a real need and desire to work harmoniously to achieve a unified purpose. You are the leader. Let them know you care. Let them know today—in words and action.

Men can naturally and without restraint talk to their officers. The products of their resourcefulness become available to all. Moreover, out of the habit  **come mutual confidence and a feeling of partnership. That's the essence of esprit de corps.**

General Dwight D. Eisenhower

The commander must practice kindness and severity and should appear friendly to the soldiers, speak to them, visit them, ask if they are well cared for, and  **alleviate their needs if they have any.**

Frederick the Great

We must have good domestic relations with ourselves before we can have good foreign relations with others.

Rabbi Joshua Loth Liebman

It is harder to win back the friendship of an offended brother than to capture a fortified city; his anger shuts you out like iron bars.

Proverbs 19:18

Regard your soldiers as your children, and they will follow you into the deepest valley. Look upon them as your own beloved sons, and they will stand by you, even unto death. If, however, you are indulgent and not  able to make your authority felt, kindhearted, but unable to enforce your commands, and incapable, moreover, of quelling disorder, then your soldiers must be likened to small children. They are useless for any practical purpose.

Sun Tsu

Leadership Secret 10

YOUR MENTOR
KEY RING

If the mountain was smooth,

you couldn't climb it.

Author Unknown

I magine a ring of magical keys. Every key represents one of your mentors. Each key provides access to a different room, town and city in your life…and in those wonderful places you will discover instruction, wisdom and adventure nearly impossible to find on your own.

In my life, there have been many mentors, starting with my parents, and then my teachers, coaches and instructors. I have been fortunate to meet people in business, government and the military who have been exemplary role models. I would not be where I am today if it were not for their contributions either by their direct instruction or by my observation of their example.

 In World War II, I had the opportunity to have a mentor and a hero as a leader, General George S. Patton. I admired him initially as much as anything for his ego and confidence. He was convinced that he was called for that time in history. I admired him for the fact that he stood up for what he thought was the best solution even when he had to pay a price for it. Now at the same time, he had his own imperfections and his ego was probably right at the top of the list. I suspect that I might have had a similar problem, as all fighter pilots do. But General Patton always stood tall. When I met him in Cherbourg, France, he came there not knowing what the results were going to be when he met with Churchill and Secretary Stinson, but he came there confident that he was destined to play a role in WWII.

In the Strategic Air Command, I once again had a mentor—another hero of mine—General Curtis LeMay. General LeMay understood who paid the price, who got the job done. He knew it was his pilots in the cockpit. All those people in between  from Wing Commanders to Squadron Command were not insignificant, but his ultimate admiration, and his ultimate, shall I say protection, was for the guy in the cockpit. That's the guy who is flying. In our particular case the B-47 was a six-engine jet airplane. He  would bypass all the middle management people, because he put all his emphasis on his aircraft commanders. We knew that, so we had confidence. He too had a humongous ego. Once, he was smoking a cigar near an airplane and a sergeant said, "General, you shouldn't be doing that. The airplane might catch on fire." His response was, "It wouldn't dare." So a strong ego also makes a good leader.

One time, I was stuck in an airplane over Morocco with a nuclear weapon on board. I could not get my gear down and was at low altitude, using up all my fuel. The tanker they sent to give me more fuel got lost. I had to either jettison the weapon or I had to land. My decision of course was to try to get the gear down. If not, I was going to jettison the weapon. The Wing Commander and everyone up the chain of command was trying to give me all kinds of advice as to what to do. Then I got a call over the high frequency radio from LeMay. He said, "Captain, you are the Aircraft Commander - the decision is yours." I knew that I had the support of the ultimate authority, the Strategic Air Command and Curtis LeMay. I admired him for that.

My training in management was primarily under the distance mentoring of Dr. Peter Drucker, who is another one of my many heroes. Dr. Drucker was a unique individual and a great teacher, however, I  never met him personally, but read everything I could find that he wrote. He was more of a manager. I was credited by a boss of mine with a compliment, when he said I had skills both in leadership and management. Generally, leaders deal with people, manager's deal with things and a pure manager or pure leader needs to have that combination. That's why you always have someone at the top and then you have the manager to straighten up the mess the guy at the top makes because he is the leader - so you need them both. I believe today that we put too much emphasis on the management aspect and educational process, and not enough on the leadership process. In the ultimate analysis, it is leaders who make the difference because they are dealing with the people rather than the things, but you need them both. If you start something on an entrepreneurial basis, it is the leader that generally starts the project, but at some point he brings in the management or it will go sour, so you need them both.

One of my most treasured mentors was a man whose leadership history was phenomenal, Dr. Frederik Philips of the Philips Corporation. He was known to his friends, employees and business associates as Fritz. He led a global enterprise with a half million employees and more than 28 billion dollars in revenue. It was a joy to know him. His book "Forty-Five Years with Philips" should be a leadership-training program in all our educational institutions. Dr. Philips was a remarkable individual, and he had a wonderful wife. He was in charge of the Philips Corporation during WWII and was pressed into handling the company because the Germans needed their products. His wife and children were placed in a concentration camp as a ransom so that he would obey the German demands. Fortunately, he and his family survived it all and never gave up their integrity. He did not have an inflated ego. For example, when he came to visit me in Atlanta, he stayed in a nice motel, but not at the Ritz-Carlton, which he could have easily afforded. Dr. Philips was very down to earth and had a good sense of humor. I asked him once how many people he had working for him. He said, "Well, I have 500,000 on the payroll, but I am not sure how many of them are working." Of course the Philips Corporation today is very much alive and well. He was a very personable person and treated me not as one beneath him, but as his equal.

You must diligently search for your own personal mentors, no matter your age or station in life. They are life's traffic cops, instructing you where to go and sometimes where to stop and take another course of action. You may need to seek them out, or they may just appear with the wisdom and direction you need. Mentors are a tremendous asset and your recognition of their value will greatly enhance your leadership skills.

When you need help climbing life's many mountains and enduring the valleys, reach for your Mentor Key Ring, select the right key, and get the help you need.

General George S. Patton
Photo taken by Mac McNair, July 1944
Cherbourg, France

The badge of rank, which an officer wears on his coat, is really a symbol of servitude to his men.

General George S. Patton

Get all the advice you can and be wise the rest of your life.

Don't forget to accept criticism. Get all the help you can.

If you refuse criticism you will end up in poverty and disgrace; but if you accept criticism you are on the road to fame.

Don't go ahead with your plans without advice from others; don't go to war until they agree.

Only a fool thinks he needs no advice, but a wise man listens to others.

The wise man is glad to be instructed, but a self-sufficient fool falls flat on his face.

Mentoring advice from the Proverbs of King Solomon

Leadership Secret 11

FROM SILVER
TO GOLD

To every person there comes that special moment
when he is tapped on the shoulder
to do a very special thing unique to him.
What a tragedy if that moment
finds him unprepared for
the work that should be his finest hour.

Winston Churchill

A good leader will grow physically, socially, academically and spiritually. Physical and mental fitness requires discipline. Social fiber is needed even though one's personality is not socially oriented. Academic growth is necessary and is based on one's goals and objectives in life. Most important of all is the spiritual dimension—what some call faith or what we might refer to as the character upon which we will base our behavior, our standards and our ethics.

Personal development is an individual matter. The simple truth is that all development is self-development. As individuals, we constantly blame outside influences for causing us to be where we are, relative to where we should be or want to be. Nevertheless, the truth is that without a goal or objective, you'll stay right where you are.

Self-development is not some complex grandiose process. It is a simple day-to-day identification of tasks to be accomplished today, tomorrow, next week and the priority for accomplishment and review of "how well did I do?"

Personal development or self-improvement applies to all of our business, personal and life goals. Your journey can be aided by reading journals, industry publications, books, and blogs. Go to seminars, take night classes, talk to experts, and join associations in your field.

You do not have to have a Ph.D. after your name to be successful, but you do need to know as much as you can about your industry, or know where to go to find out quickly, or who to go to for the answer. Decisions from a leader without knowledge can spell disaster. Opportunity does not wait for you to be ready. When preparation meets that unpredicted, random opportunity, you, your coworkers and your family reap the rewards.

Education never stops. I am still learning.

Growth is the only evidence of life.

Cardinal Newman

Little strokes fell great oaks.

Benjamin Franklin

I never let schooling interfere with my education.

Mark Twain

Let me tell you the secret that has led me to my goal. My strength lies solely in my tenacity.

Louis Pasteur

We can do anything we want to do if we stick to it long enough.

Helen Keller

EXCELLENCE AS A WAY OF LIFE

Let your heart sour as high as it will.
Refuse to be average.

A.W. Tozer

Y ou want to be an EXCELLENT leader if you have read this far. However, if your mindset and actions are generally average, you will be an average leader. Please closely focus with me on two pinnacles of personal and corporate excellence. Complete leaders live excellence.

Business leader W. B. Johnson hired me in the mid-1980's to provide management advice and help facilitate a national and global expansion of his newly acquired, several-unit hotel chain. I'm happy to report, around the world everything worked as planned, right down to the fresh pillowcases with mints on top. The worst part of advising The Ritz-Carlton: whenever a new hotel opened, I had to stay there for a long weekend!

Bill Johnson knew it takes a great team and a high standard of excellence to succeed. The difference maker was his founding president and COO Horst Schulze, who  became the heart and soul, and excellence evangelist for The Ritz-Carlton Hotel Company. Horst guided the development of a new world of elegance and personal service. The hotel industry was revolutionized. One of the most recognizable international brands was created, forever altering the very nature of customer service by creating a culture of "ladies and gentlemen serving ladies and gentlemen." Raising the bar for customer service expectations to previously unimagined levels resulted in legions of loyal customers.

Under the leadership of Bill Johnson, Horst Schulze and many others, The Ritz-Carlton won two Malcolm Baldridge National Quality Awards and set an international standard for personalized service. Now Horst is raising the bar even higher as Chairman, President and CEO of The West Paces Hotel Group. His goal? Show the world a six star standard in luxury hotels by creating an unmatched tier of customer service.

Are you leading with excellence? Are you living and breathing excellence as a way of life? Are you sure? Do those around you know it and see it?

Do you have a plan for today, this week, month, year, five years and ten years? It has been said, if you fail to plan, then you will by default, plan to fail.

The Japanese after World War II were put on the road to modernization of their manufacturing strategy when General MacArthur sent Professor Deming to teach them long range planning and other solid business principles. He is the one who gets  the credit for them being where they are today versus where we are. If you are serious about your success, you must have a strategic plan. You must ask yourself the question, "To achieve the goal I need to achieve next week, to fulfill that five year  long-range plan, what do I have to do today?" You simply lay out a timeline from today to five years - that's what you call strategic planning and that will tell you precisely what you need to do. You do not put it on the shelf and forget it - you keep it updated because it will change.

Excellence does not just happen. You must plan for it and then work with those principles daily as your way of life.

I do the very best I know how— the very best I can, and I mean to keep on doing so until the end.

Abraham Lincoln

I could use a hundred people who don't know there is such a word as impossible.

Henry Ford

If you are going to achieve excellence in big things, you develop the habit in little matters. Excellence is not an exception, it is a prevailing attitude.

General Colin Powell

Excellence is doing ordinary things extraordinarily well.

John W. Gardner

Excellence is to do a common thing in an uncommon way.

Booker T. Washington

I long to accomplish great and noble tasks, but it is my chief duty to accomplish humble tasks as though they were great and noble. The world is moved along, not only by the mighty shoves of its heroes, but also by the aggregate of tiny pushes of each honest worker.

Helen Keller

Leadership Secret 13

FLYING OVER
THE TARGET

Remember courage—moral courage,
the courage of one's convictions, the courage
to see things through. The world is in a
constant conspiracy against the brave. It's the
age-old struggle—the roar of the crowd on one side
and the voice of your conscience on the other.

General Douglas MacArthur

Courage, Loyalty and Sacrifice

F lying over a target in war takes both courage and loyalty. Leadership requires courage, loyalty and often sacrifice. An effective leader is one that is willing to fly over the target with you and for you.

National Top Secret Story #2

Mac McNair pilots a B-47 bomber.

In 1955 I was assigned to fly B-47s, 6-engine jet bombers, in the Strategic Air Command. The United States was in a war of deterrence with the Soviet Union. The objective was to prevent a nuclear war. This policy was referred to as the "John Foster Dulles Brinkmanship Diplomacy."

We would take off from the states in our B-47s, fly across the Atlantic (refueling twice in the air), coast in over Casablanca, Morocco, and then, under radio silence, continue across the Mediterranean and Black Sea into the Soviet airspace. This would alert their radar system and result in a launch of their fighter aircraft against us. However, we would reverse our flight path to preclude contact and then land at an airbase in Spain or North Africa.

This action resulted in the collapse of the Soviet Union's empire, because the communist brand of economy failed. It could not support the military build-up needed to deter our potential attacks.

 The US public was essentially unaware of this strategy and action. Only recently has it been disclosed as the so-called "Cold War". It enabled President Reagan to give his famous challenge: "Tear down this wall, Mr. Gorbachev."

I was involved in this "secret" war for four years. During this time I experienced outstanding leadership on the part of the Commanding General of the Strategic Air Command, General Curtis LeMay. He led the mission, but did not manage it.

We did that for years and got no recognition for it because it was not supposed to be happening. Quite often you don't get any recognition for some of your best accomplishments, and then if you're involved in something that gets a lot of recognition, you are likely to get the recognition, but in a delayed fashion. I received the recognition and people wondered why in the world I got it. But you don't do things for that reason - you do things because it's your responsibility and you do it. You fly over the target.

One man with courage makes a majority.

Andrew Jackson

Pain is inevitable. Suffering is optional.

Dr. H. White

There has never been a man in our history who led a life of ease whose name is worth remembering.

Theodore Roosevelt

The ideal man bears the accidents of life with dignity and grace, making the best of circumstances.

Aristotle

Courage is doing what you're afraid to do. There can be no courage unless you're scared.

Edward Vernon Rickenbacker

Courage is not simply one of the virtues, but the form of every virtue at the testing point.

C.S. Lewis

Courage is being scared to death…and saddling up anyway.

John Wayne

We can easily forgive a child who is afraid of the dark; the real tragedy of life is when men are afraid of the light.

Plato

The greatest test of courage on the earth is to bear defeat without losing heart.

R.G. Ingersoll

Leadership Secret 14

WISDOM FROM ANCIENT TEXT

I am a little pencil
in the hand of a writing God
who is sending a love letter
to the world.

Mother Teresa

Principles of Character

Since character is the most important secret to leadership, what standard do we use to measure high character? The late university professor and author Paul Kuntz passionately argued that the Ten Commandments were still the universal principles for social order and were appropriate as the basis for Twenty-First Century morality.

Difficult challenges in business and family are going to present themselves and our foundation must be built on solid, time tested principles, not man's opinions. Current events are filled with accounts of improprieties and lack of ethical behavior in every area of our culture: the government, church, education, business and family. In these uncontrolled situations of life, the need has never been greater for wisdom and knowledge of right from wrong. Daily decisions build a pattern, which reveals a person's true values. It is safe to say that we all aspire for profitability, productivity, harmony and fulfillment in all aspects of our life. If properly applied, these principles do not change with circumstances, but rather they complement rather than compete with each other to yield a full and meaningful life.

In Lincoln, Nebraska I was teaching a group of business people the decision-making process, when one of them asked the question, "How do you know your decision is the **right** one?" I responded, "You follow the decision-making process." He was not convinced. "I don't mean that," he replied. "I mean how do you know if your decision is **right** or **wrong** morally speaking?" That question led us to the 10 principles which follow.

Here are ten fundamental principles necessary for complete leadership. They are inspired from the ancient text received by Moses on Mount Sinai. Mother Teresa, one of recent history's most effective leaders, applied wisdom from ancient texts on a daily basis. We all can. If you find a better standard than the Ten Commandments for social order, character and leadership, please let me know.

ONE

Show proper respect for authority.

Authority is three-dimensional. It is down, it is up and it is collateral. The absence of authority results in chaos. Authority is a necessary prerequisite to order. Showing proper respect for authority ensures order and a climate that fosters profit.

It is necessary to show proper respect for authority, whether it is subordinate, superior or a peer level with you. Local, state, federal and foreign governments, along with family and business life, merits and deserves our respect. Proper exercise of authority is an invisible superstructure of productive enterprise.

In business, all businesses and individuals must comply with local, state, federal and foreign laws. Employees must comply with the Code of Ethics as established by the leadership of that company. Each employee must in good faith perform their duties prudently, promptly and in a professional manner.

In personal situations, each spouse must consult with the other before making significant family decisions. Respect must be shown for the other spouse's position of authority with the children. Respect should be shown to children concerning their personal belongings and bedrooms. Children should respect their siblings, their belongings and should not compete for special attention and privileges.

TWO

Have a singleness of purpose.

Effectiveness comes from activity focused on achieving a single purpose. Divided purpose dilutes effectiveness with interest conflict. No individual or company can operate effectively while trying to serve two masters. Singleness of purpose spans the use of time, talent and resources.

Integrity requires a clear understanding of personal responsibilities and values consistent and integrated with clear company responsibilities. It is wise to anticipate business, political, financial, cultural and personal influences, which would compromise the integrity of the person or the company. Any compromise would have the impact of diluting the purpose and dividing the resources. This in turn diminishes productivity and reasonable profit.

Operate your business from a written statement of purpose understood and agreed to by all employees. All business activities will be consistent with your business objectives. Use job descriptions to define each employee's responsibility, authority and standard of performance.

Align business purposes with personal purposes for a productive association with your business.

Harmonize the purpose of the business with those of the family.

THREE

Effective communication in word and deed.

Effective communication means the intended message is received, interpreted and returned to the initiator with a meaning and spirit consistent with their intent. It is a responsibility borne equally by each party and achieved when an understanding is reached. Keeping your word in the broad sense means keeping promises, pledges and oaths that include simple verbal commitments like being on time as well as completing contractual agreements. A statement of intent is a commitment that a promise will be kept in a current act or later performed on an agreed upon schedule.

Spoken and written words have a specific meaning and are not arbitrary. In the simplest form, saying "yes" means "yes" and saying "no" means "no." It means doing what you say you will do even if it is uncomfortable or inconvenient. It means telling the truth. It means the descriptions of intent are consistent with performance. It means operating with the same expectations for others. Personally, I was raised by a father who was soft-spoken. He said, "yep" or "nope." Complete communication and predictable follow-through are the basic expressions of personal integrity and the glue of profitability and success.

In business, use organizational charts to identify effective channels for communication and lines of authority. Business marketing and advertising must be truthful, tasteful and accurate. Formulate and time business communications in the best interest of the employees and customers. Business books, records and reports must be accurate, current, sufficiently detailed and truthful. Conduct regularly planned reviews of employee performance against job descriptions. Use speech and language that edifies the listener.

In your personal life, develop listening skills for your family. Practice listening skills with spouse. Communicate with your family while away from home. Teach your children conversational manners.

If you are uncomfortable speaking in front of business groups, I would encourage you to join Toastmasters International. There are chapters in most large cities. They have turned around many corporate executives who are otherwise very knowledgeable subject matter experts, into poised and articulate presenters.

Also, learn to incorporate PowerPoint into your presentations. If you are overwhelmed with the software, there are usually people in your group that are already up to speed on the program and can help you get started. Also, there are many tutorials online to help you. Even check with your children: they grasp computer skills very quickly and may have had graphics courses at their school.

FOUR

Provide proper rest, recreation and reflection for yourself and for others.

Providing proper rest, recreation and reflection are the hallmarks of free men and free enterprise. They are the celebration of the prerogatives of free and responsible men under God. They are requirements for maximized creativity, productivity and motivations.

The work ethic produces a quality service and product. Rest is a necessity for effectiveness. Recreation guards the mind against mental and emotional fatigue. Reflection closes the gap by which meaning is pressed into work and ensures single-mindedness. The knowledge, creativity and commitment of employees directly relates not only to their health, but also to the productivity and profitability of the organization. Proper rest, recreation and reflection ensure quality of life as well as profitability and safety in the workplace.

In business, strive to provide adequate staff for anticipated workload. Schedule breaks, vacations, shifts and days off to produce individual and team effectiveness. Plan sufficient rest periods to maximize safety, productivity and effectiveness. Schedule appropriate and periodic times for reflection and planning for personal and business activity. Build time for reflection into the job description proportionate to the responsibility of each employee.

Provide leadership for your family to devote a day to worship. Provide recreational activities for your family. Teach your family a work ethic that will accomplish assigned tasks. Teach your family how to plan.

FIVE

Show respect for elders.

Many have shared directly or indirectly in the development of our culture and the opportunities afforded to us as individuals. Parents, teachers, coaches, soldiers and working associates have an investment in us. It is to our benefit to honor that investment and draw fully from their wisdom and expertise of the greater experience.

Ethics are more caught than taught, i.e. children seeing how you behave rather than, "Do as I say, rather than as I do." This always leaves a more permanent impression.

Parents teach their children and their children's children. Historically, mentors are older men teaching the younger men, and older women teaching the younger women. Tradition, coupled with strong relationships and a personal understanding of why we do what we do, is the best training. Lessons in profitability from the past are protections of profitability in the future.

In business, seek the counsel of those with great experience. Honor the culture, traditions and customs of those with whom you do business. Anticipate situations which may be customary practice, but which may compromise you legally or morally. Employ older, seasoned individuals as leaders and role models in teaching the nuances of ethical business protocol and conduct. Comply with laws regarding non-discrimination on the basis of age.

Assume responsibility to care for parents. Teach your children to respect their elders. Show your children that your spouse is a very high priority.

SIX

Show respect for human life, dignity and rights.

The value of human life and worth of an individual are pivotal concepts to long-term leadership and profitability. They obviously apply to every level of human relationship. One's relationship with God, family, associates, constituents, and your self-image demand morally right attitudes and right actions. They encompass product quality, service, work environment, health, safety, personnel policies, responsibilities, and competitive practices.

These are only highlights: the value of human life and the worth of the individual are the underlying issues of our laws. The concept may be as simple as living by the Golden Rule, "treating people as you would want to be treated." Respect for the individual gives us confidence and freedom to perform at our highest level of creativity, energy and productivity. It is the hallmark of a leader.

In business, apply the "Golden Rule" as the fundamental criteria for decision-making. Conduct all operations in a manner which protects the health and safety of employees. Establish personnel policies that acknowledge the uniqueness of all individuals. Make all employees aware that character, competence and demonstrated conviction are rewarded. Adhere to a clearly defined, written hiring/firing policy based on regard for the dignity of the individual. State employee conditions at the onset of employment.

Respect the dignity of your spouse and children. Do not physically, emotionally or verbally abuse them. Control your anger when discipline is necessary. Teach your children equality of race and national origin.

SEVEN

Maintain a stability of the sexes and the family.

Marital fidelity is fundamental to the success of a family unit. A family functions best when both spouses contribute 100% (not "50/50"), love each other without condition and take full responsibility for their actions. Parents must expect their children to honor them. Marriage and singleness are equally honorable. A publicly committed marriage of a man and a woman is a desirable institution.

Children are a desirable benefit of that union and an invaluable asset to the relationship.

The family unit is a greenhouse for growing commitments, convictions, communications, companionship and a personal value system. The basic unit of society is a man, woman and a baby. Leadership training begins in the home. A fundamental institution in every culture and society is the family unit.

Historically, when the family has been recognized and respected, the culture has enjoyed stability and longevity. Both in and outside of marriage, when the sexual uniqueness and responsibility of men and women are ignored or perverted, the culture fails.

Therefore, a person in business is faced with a crucial and fragile leadership issue. On one hand, respect for the family structure and the unique responsibility of men as husbands and women as wives are prerequisites for long-term profitability, even when business demands seem to compete with family and personal life.

Yet, on the other hand, wisdom and good business practice dictate equal regard for men and women as persons irrespective of gender or marital status.

This is the case when matching any person—man or woman—to any job: consideration must be given to all emotional, spiritual, physical, psychological, and intellectual strengths and weaknesses.

In business, sexual relationships outside of marriage, even when legal, are unacceptable for a productive association with your business. Seek counsel and expect aggressive business involvement and discipline. Every individual has the fundamental priority and responsibility for a strong home life. Parents have the ultimate responsibility for their family members. Corporate policies should offer equal employment opportunity for men and women and should respect the uniqueness and dignity of each individual. Management decisions involving workload, deadlines, quotas and travel scheduling should be made in light of personal, marriage and family needs. Single persons will not be discriminated against or treated with more or less dignity than married persons.

You must maintain the fidelity of your spousal relationship. Failure to do so will result in long term erosion of your personal, emotional, financial and business wellbeing. Be a role model for your friends and coworkers concerning the sanctity of marriage. Teach your children the sanctity of the covenant of marriage, respect for the opposite sex and equality of the sexes.

EIGHT

Demonstrate proper allocation of resources.

There are two fundamental responsibilities and privileges of leadership: the optimum use of material resources and wise leadership of people. To the degree that materials are misused and people improperly led, productivity and profitability suffer. So, proper allocation of natural resources and raw materials require a commitment not to steal from future generations.

Pollution and improper handling of hazardous and toxic materials may cut costs in the short-run but fuel a staggering deficit for everyone in the long-run. Company profits, funds and assets must be protected and managed well to prevent theft.

All constituents have a responsibility to manage resources well. A leader realizes the need for proper utilization of personnel resources as well. A person whose interest and ability are matched with job function will not only realize satisfaction at work, but will also make a maximum contribution to the company.

In business, every individual is responsible to manage the materials entrusted to them. Bills must be paid promptly and consistently with vendor agreements. Business property, assets and information must not be used for personal benefit except by proper agreement. Refrain from offering, pursuing or accepting bribes or kickbacks. Maximal development and regard for each individual's wellbeing, motivations and competence is a business priority. Operations will comply with environmental regulations with a bent toward improvement.

Teach your children the value of managing resources, financial responsibility and avoiding debt. Teach your children to respect our natural resources and participate in environmental projects. Role model the principle of giving.

NINE

Demonstrate honesty and integrity.

A reputation for honesty is a comprehensive statement of both a person's character and how they treat others. The fundamental mindset against stealing, lying and deceiving requires a willingness to deal with facts and guard others from fraud. Integrity is the cornerstone of any good relationship.

Without demonstrating the willingness to give and the worthiness to receive trust, no business or relationship can survive or prosper. Personal honesty and integrity are the fundamental building blocks for profitability, effective management and harmonious relationships. Say what you mean and mean what you say.

In business, do what is truthful rather than what is expedient. If asked to do something dishonest, disclose the situation immediately to the proper director or officer. Prepare records and reports accurately, truthfully and in sufficient detail to describe the actual transactions. Do not engage in any wrongful activity in order to maintain or enhance your personal or company reputation. Do what is right and your reputation will follow. Do not engage in any activity that would adversely affect the reputation or an associate or competitor. Honor commitments and show respect for the time of others by being on time.

Honor your spouse and children by keeping your commitments and promises; be a promise keeper. Teach children to tell the truth. Do not gossip. Be home for dinner on time. If you cannot be home on time, call and let your spouse know your schedule and why you are being detained.

TEN

The right of property ownership.

The free enterprise system benefits those who perform, are disciplined, creative, prudent and industrious. They are entitled to the fruits of their labor. The most satisfied person in the workplace, whether employer or employee, maintains honorable relationships with his family, associates and constituents. They operate with the view that they are unique as a person and have an ultimate contribution to make to the business world. Their focus is on developing the full potential of their intellect, character, skills and gifts and employing them in productive work.

Content with themselves and what they have, any prestige, power and wealth are a result of their productivities and not their ambitions. Their goals of personal responsibility for maximizing their own profitability are synergistic contributions to the company team.

In business, manage your resources and assets toward promoting and protecting the free enterprise system, self-regulation and voluntary compliance. Design salaries, wages and benefits for each employee as compensations for performance and as an incentive for increased productivity. Reward innovation, initiative, advancements in competence and community involvement consistent with the values expressed in this code.

Maintain a lifestyle that is not "keeping up with the Jones." Respect your neighbor's property. Teach your children personal responsibility, the free enterprise system and to become responsible community citizens.

The ability to recognize and develop these ten principles and one's personal character is the key to leadership. The leader must be willing to say to the person that is being led, "These are the principles you can hold me accountable to and these are the principles I will hold you accountable to."

These principles are applicable to every aspect of our lives. They level the playing field in family, business, education, church, government and all of the social institutions. The foundational principles ensure that objectives, actions schedules and resources are consistent with the purpose of the business and family organization. The end results never justify the means for accomplishment. When people and their skills are abused or misused, the entire planning process suffers. The principled plans include the institutions objective, based on established values and priorities. The proper execution of these principles results in a stable family, business and society. To perfect these principles is a life's work and takes persistent dedication. The journey is worth the effort.

Biblical Commandment	Business Commandment
"I am the Lord your God… You shall have no other gods before Me."	Show proper respect for authority.
"You shall not make for yourself an idol."	Have singleness of purpose.
"You shall not misuse the name of the Lord your God."	Use effective communication in word and deed.
"Remember the Sabbath day by keeping it holy."	Provide proper rest, recreation and reflection.
"Honor your father and your mother, so that you may live long…"	Show respect for elders.
"You shall not murder."	Show respect for human life, dignity and rights.
"You shall not commit adultery."	Maintain stability of the sexes and the family.
"You shall not steal."	Demonstrate proper allocation of resources.
"You shall not give false testimony…"	Demonstrate honesty and integrity.
"You shall not covet…"	Maintain the right of ownership of property.

Leadership Secret 15

Lead!

Do it.

Do it right.

Do it now.

N.A.S.A. slogan

Importance of action.

Leaders must LEAD! All of the world's knowledge and education is worthless without application. There is no finer example of a decisive, complete leader for a lifetime than my friend, the late General Joe Foss.

"The story of Joe Foss's life is a story of human endeavor so great and so accomplished that it defies exaggeration," said Senator John McCain. Paul Harvey reported that only Joe Foss has gone to the top of four unrelated professions. You can be a Joe Foss.

Foss was destined to be a pilot from that day in 1926, when at age 11 he attended an air show in Sioux Falls, South Dakota that featured aviator Charles Lindbergh. After watching Lindy perform, the young man was hooked.

He graduated from the University of South Dakota in 1940 with both a business degree and a civilian pilot's license.

On October 9, 1942, Foss and his fighter wing found themselves at Henderson Field on Guadalcanal. His two four-plane group would eventually come to be called, "Foss's Flying Circus" and would fly over 60 missions. On October 16, he shot down two Japanese Zeros and a bomber, to bring his total kills to five, and making him an "Ace" in just a week. By mid-November, Foss's personal total of downed Japanese planes stood at 19 while he had been shot down once himself. He had also won the Distinguished Flying Cross.

Foss was called back to Washington, in May, 1943 to help lead the campaign for U.S. War Bonds. He found himself on the cover of *Life* magazine when President Franklin Roosevelt presented him with the nation's highest award, the Congressional Medal of Honor for   outstanding heroism above and beyond the call of duty during his entire time on Guadalcanal. In part his citation read: "His remarkable flying skill, inspiring leadership, and indomitable fighting spirit were distinctive factors in the defense of strategic American positions on Guadalcanal."

Joe embodied all of the timeless, proven principles in *Leadership-15 Secrets Revealed.* He led his entire life when others could not or would not and led regardless of the challenges or setbacks. Joe was a leader. He was Joe regardless of who he was with, he was Joe.

I was honored to have my friend Joe Foss as keynote speaker at my initial announcement function as candidate for Governor of Georgia.

Joe's actions changed his world and ours. Your actions can do the same, in your own personal way. Joe understood Will Roger's advice: "Even though you're on the right track, you'll get run over if you just sit there."

IN SUMMARY

APPLICATION! APPLICATION!

Application is an essential ingredient for leadership. Principles do not work without application.

General Patton said, "Lead, follow, or get the hell out of the way".

Do not form a committee. Act and apologize later. A committee is the greatest stumbling block to the advancement of mankind. Committees do not lead, individuals do. Institutions do not lead, individuals do.

Leaders apply the principles and the actions produce results. President Kennedy said, "Man on the moon by 1970." Action based on principles achieved the goal in 1969.

As quoted about my former commander General Curtis LeMay: "Time after time he led his bombers through storms of German flack and bullets." As a Strategic Air Commander, he led the air force that destroyed Russia in the Cold War.

When I was in an emergency situation in Morocco with a Mark-15 nuclear bomb on board, and receiving conflicting orders from the control tower, General LeMay's voice came over the radio: "Captain McNair, you are the aircraft commander – the decision is yours." Action is the final key to leadership.

Everyone can lead – regardless of age, activity, profession, circumstance, season and station in life. The secrets and rewards of leadership have now been revealed. All of the tools are in your mind and heart. Just one thing left to do: LEAD!

If not us, then who? If not now, then when?

President Ronald W. Reagan

If you put everything off till you're sure of it, you'll get nothing done.

Norman Vincent Peale

The difference between a successful person and others is not a lack of strength, not a lack of knowledge, but rather a lack of will.

Vince Lombardi

A public-opinion poll is no substitute for thought. Risk is a part of God's game, alike for men and nations.
Risk comes from not knowing what you're doing.

Warren Buffett

As we look ahead into the next century, leaders will be those who empower others.
It's fine to celebrate success, but it is more important to heed the lessons of failure.

Bill Gates

My legacy isn't what I do on the football field. It's what I say and do when people don't see me.

Tom Dungy
Winning Super Bowl Coach

Afterword

Lifelong
<u>Leadership</u>

Anyone who stops learning is old,
whether at twenty or eighty.
Anyone who keeps learning stays young.
The greatest thing in life
is to keep your mind young.

Henry Ford

L eaders never retire. I will celebrate my 88th birthday soon and there is still much I want to accomplish. One of the evils of our culture, which destroys and eliminates leaders, is what we refer to as retirement. The responsibility of leaders is to mentor future generations by living and sharing the principles and keys to leadership.

Retirement is not healthy! Life insurance statistics show that people who retire and live sedentary lives, rocking on the front porch, many times die within two years of leaving the workforce. Stay active! Pursue your dreams! Start your own business. Get involved with your grandchildren, church and community. Work at your own pace, but work at something! Pursuit of your vision is the zest of life.

 Colonel Harland Sanders formed his nationwide Kentucky Fried Chicken chain when he was seventy! He received the Horatio Alger Award at seventy-five! That award is given to "community leaders who demonstrate individual initiative and a commitment to excellence—as exemplified by remarkable achievements accomplished through honesty, hard work, self-reliance, and perseverance."

 All award members "have a strong commitment to assisting those less fortunate than themselves (mentoring) and a loyalty and devotion to American ideals and the American free enterprise system."

Live until you die!

Rev. Dr. Frank Harrington
Former Senior Pastor of the largest
Presbyterian Church in the United States
and Europe.

The saddest words of tongue or pen are these four words— it might have been.

U.S. Supreme Court Justice
Oliver Wendell Holmes

As to that leisure evening of life, I must say that I do not want it. I can conceive of no contentment of which toil is not to be the immediate parent.

Anthony Trollope
Prominent English Novelist

I believe that work is a gift, not a curse. Work is part of the reason why you and I are still alive. We still have things to accomplish.

Michael Hyatt
Chairman of Thomas Nelson Publishers

Col. McNair in the Vietnam War, 1968

Join me in the fun of lifelong leadership!

120

EXECUTIVE LEADERSHIP FOUNDATION

A 501(c) tax exempt, non-profit organization

9245 Creekside Trail
Stone Mountain, GA 30087

678-684-3920   770-378-7022

Email: nimrodmcnair@gmail.com

www.executiveleadershipfoundation.org